creating your perfect
CHRISTMAS

creating your perfect
CHRISTMAS

stylish ideas and step-by-step projects for the festive season

Antonia Swinson

with projects by **Sania Pell**

RYLAND
PETERS
& SMALL
LONDON NEW YORK

SENIOR DESIGNER Isabel de Cordova
SENIOR EDITOR Clare Double
PICTURE AND LOCATION RESEARCH Emily Westlake
PRODUCTION Gemma Moules
ART DIRECTOR Anne-Marie Bulat
PUBLISHING DIRECTOR Alison Starling

First published in the United States in 2006 by
Ryland Peters & Small
519 Broadway, 5th Floor
New York, NY 10012
www.rylandpeters.com

10 9 8 7 6 5 4 3 2

Printed and bound in China

Library of Congress Cataloging-in-Publication Data

Swinson, Antonia.
    Creating your perfect Christmas : stylish ideas and step-
by-step projects for the festive season / Antonia Swinson
with projects by Sania Pell.
        p. cm.
    ISBN-13: 978-1-84597-256-1
    ISBN-10: 1-84597-256-2
    1. Christmas decorations. 2. Handicraft. I. Pell, Sania.
II. Title.
    TT900.C4S95 2006
    745.594'12–dc22
                                    2006007884

contents

Introduction

Christmas is a time for traditions, but not just the ones we all share—
the tree, the meal, the stockings. There are also the traditions that
evolve within families, such as the day on which the tree is decorated;
the arrangement of candles that is always placed on the front windowsill;
and the little wooden angels that have adorned the mantelpiece for
years. Many of these cherished rituals revolve around decorations, and
handmade ones tend to have a particularly special meaning. There may
be stockings knitted and embroidered by a grandmother; or a clothespin
angel for the top of the tree we made as a child.

This book is full of ideas for ways to decorate every part of the house,
some based on purchased ornaments, but most featuring makes that
are within the grasp of anyone with the inclination and patience to try
them. Many of the materials used can be bought in any mall, while others
are readily available from craft stores and mail-order suppliers. There are
also a number of inspiring craft projects that employ surprisingly simple
techniques to produce unusual and beautiful objects. Moreover, many of
the ideas shown here are ideal for children to get involved in, such as
cards, gift tags, beaded baubles, and paper snowflakes. So be inspired,
try things out, and above all, have fun.

Advent calendars and stockings

A simple homemade advent calendar—perhaps no more than painted and numbered matchboxes hanging from a collection of branches—that is brought out lovingly every year will repay your efforts many times. Handmade stockings are also sure to become much-loved objects whose annual appearance is eagerly anticipated. A little time and patience is all that's required, and since felt and trims can be glued on, you don't even need to sew them.

advent calendars

The mounting excitement of counting the days to Christmas with a special calendar has been a seasonal ritual since the nineteenth century. The familiar pictures behind little doors are the most common, but more imaginative versions are great fun for children. Begin with a few branches from your garden or a florist. Hang up anything that can be numbered—miniature stockings, tiny envelopes, craft boxes, fabric bags, paper cones, or painted matchboxes—and fill with chocolates, little toys, or a seasonal "Did you know…?" Alternatively, use ribbon to hang your containers from window and door frames or the mantelpiece, or try a board with pegs or hooks, to which luggage labels, gift tags, or envelopes can be hung together with a present or keepsake.

ABOVE AND FAR RIGHT Baby socks, spotted with felt dots and hung from branches, form a quirky advent calendar. You could also use tiny mittens.

ABOVE RIGHT Numbered luggage tags make a simple, inexpensive display to which gifts—here, a tiny gold organza cracker—can be attached.

Hang up anything that can be numbered—miniature stockings, tiny envelopes, craft boxes, fabric bags, paper cones, or painted matchboxes—and fill.

ABOVE LEFT Diminutive galvanized buckets (look in florists) create a homey advent calendar. Tied with gingham ribbon and lined with scraps of pretty fabric, they hang in rows from a mantelpiece.

ABOVE RIGHT A panel of hooks is the starting point for this advent calendar of numbered, beribboned tags and brightly wrapped parcels.

FAR LEFT White boxes (available from craft suppliers), tied with gold braid and hung from gold-sprayed branches, make an understated and sophisticated advent calendar.

PROJECT 1
jingle bells advent calendar

This jolly advent calendar, complete with shiny bells to signal raiding fingers, will be a treat to bring out year after year. Using felt or another non-fray fabric for the background and numbers makes life easy and will mean that the finished calendar looks neat and wears well. If you can't face sewing on the numbers, they could be glued. As for color, a combination of red and white will give the hanging a Nordic look; white, cool red, and soft blue will lend it a vintage, Shaker style; or you could choose an unconventional but fun mixture of vibrant colors such as red, pink, orange, and yellow. Whatever you choose, children will love having their own unique countdown to Christmas.

MATERIALS & EQUIPMENT
felt for background • contrasting non-fray fabric such as felt or suedette for roof • swatches of fabric for pockets, numbers, etc.
sequins and sequin stars
embroidery thread
dowel
ribbon
small bells
paper for patterns • pencil • carpenter's square
pins • needle • cotton thread • scissors • tape measure

1 Mark a rectangle for the "house" on the back of the felt using a pencil and carpenter's square. Our cream felt base was 39 in (1 m) long and 16½ in (42 cm) wide. Cut out. Draw the roof shape on the back of the contrasting fabric and cut out.

2 Cut out 23 pieces of fabric, about 3 x 2½ in (7.5 cm x 6 cm), for the pockets, and one larger piece. Cut paper patterns for numbers 1 to 9, a star, and a snowflake (templates on page 108). Pin onto non-fray fabric, cut out, and pin onto pockets.

3 Stitch numbers from 1 to 23 onto the pocket pieces, and 24 on the larger piece for the front door. Add stars, snowflakes, and a few sequins. Sew the pockets onto the felt house in random order, using contrasting embroidery thread.

4 Sew on felt plant pots, with a line of running stitch for fir-tree trunks, and "branches" of stitches, as shown. Fold over the top of the house and stitch in a dowel; tie ribbon around this to hang. Last, add bells and fill the pockets.

ABOVE Felt is ideal for all sorts of Christmas projects, including appliquéd stockings such as this one, since it doesn't fray and comes in every color.

RIGHT These modern, funky stockings have been run up from thick corduroy, edged with shaggy fake fur. Simple motifs have been embroidered in running stitch.

stockings

Those of us who remember waking to feel a stocking lying across the end of the bed and the thrill of all the intriguing little parcels it contained know why stockings are the best thing about Christmas morning. Popularized by the Victorians, their origins reach back to the real, fourth-century Saint Nicholas, who left coins for the poor in their socks and shoes.

You'll find stockings for sale everywhere, but they're so easy and satisfying to make that it seems a shame not to make your own. Take a real sock as your reference for shape, enlarged to the right size (don't skimp, because even

FAR LEFT A thoughtful present for a house guest, this miniature stocking will hold a few chocolates or a special trinket.

LEFT For adults, stockings are enjoyable and satisfying to create. For children, they'll become a cherished part of their yearly festive ritual.

ABOVE If you're not skilled with a needle, make a basic stocking and glue on ready-made embroidered motifs, tiny wooden toys, sequins, ribbon, braid, or beads. With a couple of easy stitches such as chain or blanket stitch, you can embroider initials or simple seasonal shapes.

RIGHT In a nod to Shaker style, this stocking is in simple white, blue, and red.

FAR RIGHT Striking a boho note, this stocking is made from remnants of embroidery and velvet, and drips with beads.

OPPOSITE, BELOW A handmade patchwork stocking is a labor of love. Here, fabrics in traditional checks and stripes give a vintage look.

Fabric and craft stores stock festive material over the season. In a more exotic vein, rich brocade, velvet, or satin will make a stocking fit for a king.

small presents take up a surprising amount of space). Felt is ideal as it's cheap, colorful, and frayproof. Otherwise, fabric and craft stores stock festive material over the season, or try cotton gingham. In a more exotic vein, rich brocade, velvet, or satin will make a stocking fit for a king. If you can't sew, opt for felt and simply use glue. Names, initials, and motifs can be embroidered on with the simplest of stitches—running, chain, or blanket—and shapes can be appliquéd (felt is also a good choice here). Other embellishments might include ribbon, braid, beads, or sequins. If you're a knitter, use up your yarn remnants by scaling up a basic sock pattern and making one in exuberant stripes. For a knitted effect without the effort, cut stockings out of old sweaters, overlocking raw edges on a sewing machine so that they don't fray.

ABOVE AND FAR LEFT In many families, sacks rather than stockings bulge with presents on Christmas morning. Here, a burlap sack is trimmed with gingham and satin ribbon. Alternatively, find an old white pillowcase, buy some fabric crayons from a craft store, and let children decorate it themselves. Or make hat stockings—like elongated pixie hats, with a bell on the end.

PROJECT 2
vintage stocking

This vintage-style boot is a glamorous, girlie reworking of a traditional stocking. For this design choose a luxurious fabric such as satin, silk, or taffeta, in a soft feminine shade such as ballet-shoe pink, ice blue, pistachio, or champagne. Keep color contrasts, in the form of felt and embroidery threads, gentle so that the effect is unashamedly pretty. Mismatched buttons, perhaps pearly or sparkly in finish, will add a touch of quirkiness. If you want to give your lace a slightly aged look in keeping with the vintage theme, try dipping it in strong cold tea.

MATERIALS & EQUIPMENT
tracing paper for templates (see page 109)
fabric for boot shape
felt in a contrasting color
embroidery threads
sequins
lace to decorate top ruffle
assorted buttons
ribbon
pins • needle • cotton thread • scissors

1 Cut out templates for the boot shape. To go on the boot front, cut templates for the heel and toe tips, top ruffle, and flowers and leaves. Pin onto fabric for the front and back of the boot, and felt for the other shapes. Carefully cut out.

2 Pin the leaves, flowers, heel and toe, and top ruffle on the front boot shape. Sew on using small running stitch. Stitch "veins" on the leaves using contrasting embroidery thread. Sew on sequins to make flower centers and add sparkle.

3 Pin the front and back boot pieces together. Using contrasting thread, backstitch the boot together, keeping the stitches even. Pin and stitch lace onto the top ruffle, taking care not to sew the boot closed.

4 Stitch around the heel and toe areas using contrasting embroidery thread. Add different-size buttons along the front edge for decoration. Sew a ribbon "handle" at the top of the boot to hang the stocking up on Christmas Eve.

Decorative displays

Decking the halls of medieval homes meant bringing inside boughs of evergreens such as holly and ivy, winter berries, and mistletoe. Such is the strength of Christmas traditions that natural materials and motifs still play a significant role in the way we prepare our homes for the festivities. We also have a vast array of other decorations at our disposal, allowing us to adopt a particular style—traditional or modern, rustic or urban, colorful or subdued—or to invent one all of our own.

Red and green, the colors of winter berries and evergreen foliage, are a classic combination.

traditional

We have the Victorians to thank for many of our traditional Christmas decorations, and we are inspired by the rich colors and formality of the nineteenth century at this time of year. Red and green, the colors of winter berries and evergreen foliage, are a classic combination and, with touches of gold or silver, create the right sense of drama and opulence. For this look you might choose a tree laden with ornate red and gold balls, heavy damask table linen, chunky candles, tartan stockings hanging from the mantelpiece, and darkest red roses or frosted fruits. For a traditional look in a more adventurous palette, try combining ruby red, plum, purple, and burgundy, highlighted with silver or copper.

OPPOSITE The inclusion of sprayed twigs in the centerpiece gives a modern slant to this classic red and gold table setting.

OPPOSITE INSET Ready-to-decorate styrofoam balls can be bought from craft suppliers. This one has been covered with seed heads.

BELOW LEFT These gold letters hanging in the branches of a house plant would also look good propped up on a mantelpiece or shelf.

BELOW RIGHT An old-fashioned candy jar displays ornate glass balls that look almost good enough to eat.

Red and white—fire and ice—are the key colors and make this a fresh and bright look.

CENTER LEFT Many traditional Scandinavian decorations are made by families at home. Here, corn umbrellas, gingerbread shapes, painted wooden ornaments, fabric hearts, and clothespin Santa Clauses adorn the tree.

LEFT A tiny bag hangs on a children's advent tree.

BOTTOM LEFT AND BELOW Classic Nordic red and white make for a bright, light scheme. Bottom left, a circle of corn dolls hangs from red ribbon.

nordic

The Scandinavian style of decorating the home for Christmas is charmingly understated and homespun. Red and white—fire and ice—are the key colors and help to make this a fresh and bright look. Traditional decorations are often made from wood or corn, focusing on simple motifs such as stars and hearts, and families bake gingerbread cookies to hang on the tree. Scandinavian homes are filled with candles during Advent, and candles (both real and electric, as seen on page 33) and stylized wooden figures are often placed in windows to be seen from outside. Bulbs such as narcissi and hyacinths, forced into early flowering, fill rooms with scent. Table settings are homey rather than elaborate and often feature a gingham tablecloth or runner, embroidered napkins, and white china.

ABOVE LEFT This striking centerpiece of bare twigs and glowing red berries is hung with painted wooden shapes including hearts and angels.

TOP RIGHT A bowl of twigs, berries, and headily scented hyacinths suggests the hope of spring after a long winter.

ABOVE CENTER This wooden dove is hung with lavender-filled fabric hearts.

ABOVE A woven-corn umbrella rests on a napkin kept specially for Christmas.

BOTTOM Hips from a rambler rose, placed in a tumbler, bring a dash of intense color indoors.

BELOW This galvanized bucket greets visitors in the hall. The beeswax tapers (which burn longer than standard paraffin candles) are anchored in sand.

RIGHT A wreath of artificial berries has been customized with bows of red satin ribbon and narrower plaid ribbon.

BELOW RIGHT Ginger cookies can be hung from the tree or presented to guests.

country

For centuries, people have decorated their homes with evergreens, mistletoe, and other plants at Christmas time. Handmade decorations, muted colors, and seasonal foliage and fruits play important roles in the rustic look. Bowls of pot pourri, pine cones, and clove-studded citrus pomanders provide the woody and spicy scents of the season. Homespun tree ornaments include gingerbread hearts, gold-sprayed pine cones, styrofoam balls covered with dried flower petals, and garlands of dried orange slices. Candles, perhaps in ivy-trimmed jars, create a welcoming atmosphere, while evergreen boughs and holly bring the outside inside. For the table, arrangements of apples, berries, and foliage set a rustic tone.

At Christmas time handmade decorations,
muted colors, and seasonal foliage and fruits
play important roles in the rustic look.

With a bit of imagination,
humble ingredients can be
given a new lease on life. Here,
styrofoam stars (available from
craft suppliers) have been
covered with red mung beans.

RIGHT A glitter ball, nestling in a length of fairy lights, will add a bit of retro fun to a Christmas interior.

FAR RIGHT Milky glass beakers, perhaps waiting to be filled with nutmeg-laced eggnog, stand on a runner made of handmade Japanese paper embossed with circles.

OPPOSITE TOP LEFT These clear glass balls, hung from a window to form a "curtain," have feathers suspended inside.

BELOW Feather butterflies, patterned with glitter, are a beautiful addition to a beaded-wire garland.

RIGHT A family of polar bears strides along a mantelpiece on which a fantastical winter scene has been created with paper snowflakes, green-bead trees, and white feathers.

whites

An all-white decorating scheme needn't be minimalist. When color is monotone, texture and pattern become all-important. Offset white with silver, gold, iridescence, and transparency. A tree of white-sprayed branches could be hung with pearly shells, glass icicles, sequined snowflakes, and silver balls. Shiny, reflective decorations and flickering votive candles or twinkling fairy lights will enhance each other. Anchor white tapers in glass nuggets, or intersperse pillar candles with chalky pebbles. Hang tissue-paper snowflakes in windows or make into garlands. Set the table with white linen and china, then arrange a string of fairy lights down the center, pile clear and frosted balls in dishes, tie napkins with white satin ribbon and feathers, and place votives in tiny white pots.

TOP CENTER A wire wreath of glass beads and paper flowers frames a white pillar candle.

TOP RIGHT This chandelier-style tree decoration, with light-catching glass droplets, is both elegant and whimsical.

ABOVE Displaying glass votives on a round mirror maximizes the soft glow of the candlelight.

LEFT This white-sprayed tree is in fact a bare Christmas tree, which has been rescued and reused. Extra twigs were added to give it a fuller look, then it was hung with handmade paper snowflakes and clear glass balls.

PROJECT 3
rose, berry, and ivy pomander

Velvety blood-red roses and brilliant red berries give this floral ball a luxurious, sophisticated look. Roses are always reliable for flower arranging because they have such a sculptural form and last well once cut, too. This technique for making a pomander can also be used with other flowers and plant material. Try dried flowers and seed heads, perhaps sprayed gold or silver, or carnations (which have strong stems and come in sumptuous dark reds and pinks). If you choose roses, you could experiment with misting them with metallic spray, or even lightly applying spray-on glue, then sprinkling on glitter.

MATERIALS & EQUIPMENT
oasis ball 5–6 in (12–15 cm) diameter
fine wire
about 30 roses
berry stalks
small dish or bowl
thin ribbon in a color to contrast with the roses
ivy
wire or hairpins
scissors

1 Tie wire around the center of the oasis ball. Make two loops of the wire, opposite each other, to give you something to attach the hanging ribbons to. Trim the rose stalks and berry stems to approximately 6 in (15 cm) long.

2 Support the oasis ball on a bowl to leave both hands free to work with. Starting at the top, push the rose stems in evenly and position the berry stalks between. Pick up with care and insert roses and berries over the rest of the ball.

3 Tie a long hanging loop of ribbon to the top wire loop. Tie several shorter lengths of ribbon to the bottom wire loop, as shown. Take care not to crush the roses—you may find it easier to hang the ball first, then attach the bottom ribbons.

4 Trail ivy around the top ribbon and secure in place with wire or hairpins. Finally, water the oasis lightly using a watering can with a thin spout. Take care not to overwater, which could cause the wire to cut through the oasis ball.

OPPOSITE This elegant wooden mantelpiece has been sympathetically decorated with painted wooden horses and Santas. Richly colored glass balls hang below from gingham ribbon.

LEFT As a safe alternative to real candles, this wooden stand of painted animals comes with electric versions.

BELOW Real or fake candles are a welcoming sight on a windowsill, where they can be seen by approaching guests or passers-by. Here, plain white candles of different sizes are turned into a still life with the addition of fir-tree branches.

room decorations

A mantelpiece is the traditional place to hang up stockings, but if your children favor the end of the bed you might want to frame your fireplace with a swag or garland instead. You could also attach a line of cord or ribbon and hang on your prettiest cards (be careful they don't hang too low if you're going to light a real fire). Try candles or votives on the shelf, particularly if you have a mirror above to reflect the light, along with foliage, pine cones, fruit, or roses. You could also place a wreath here; create a display with your prettiest balls; or arrange a nativity scene.

Windowsills are ideal for a display to welcome visitors, so candles are an obvious choice here. If they're deep enough, windowsills also lend themselves to nativity scenes

RIGHT This choir of angels is suspended from a staircase on fishing line. The angels are made from clothespins, with scraps of fabric and paper for clothes, and skeleton leaves (from craft suppliers) for wings.

BELOW RIGHT Frosted fruits (see page 76) can be piled onto dishes, or interspersed with candles on a platter for an impressive centerpiece.

FAR RIGHT Homemade organdy stockings, filled with pot pourri, make an unusual feature hung from a chandelier.

BELOW Children enjoy making paper or tissue snowflakes (see page 47). Here, they've been stuck to a window.

and even small trees, perhaps decorated to echo the main tree elsewhere in the house.

We tend to focus on decorating our reception rooms, usually giving pride of place in one of them to the tree. However, don't forget the rest of your living space. Halls are on show as soon as you open the front door, and are useful for displaying cards, while staircases are good places to hang garlands or little figures. The kitchen is the scene of many of our Christmas preparations, and decorating it helps to make it a merry setting for our labors. Children love to help with decorations, so why not let them have free rein in their bedrooms, giving them miniature trees, fairy lights, and paper chains? Let them do the spare bedroom, too, if you're hosting guests—a guaranteed way to make them feel welcome.

ABOVE Gold candles and gold-sprayed pebbles make a glamorous and modern display for a hearth or mantelpiece. This look could also be created using ordinary votive candles and white pebbles, glass nuggets, or white gravel.

ABOVE CENTER AND RIGHT White fairy lights have become a Christmas classic, but strings of lights are now available in a host of shapes and colors. These rather sophisticated lights have shades made to resemble skeleton leaves.

ABOVE RIGHT Inexpensive everyday objects can be recycled and turned into stylish decorations. Here, glass jars are transformed into pretty, ivy-trimmed candle holders.

festive winter mobile

This mobile, bedecked with wooden stars and hearts, feathers, skeleton leaves, and pine cones, is an answer to some of the brasher, glitzier elements of Christmas decoration. With its accent on natural materials and muted colors, it uses motifs and textures in a simple, rustic way, although it would look just as good in a modern, minimalist interior as it would in a country hallway. Although the leaves, pine cones, and feathers are all available to buy, it might be fun to set children the task of finding them in the garden or on a country walk or stroll in the park. As a final touch, attach some mistletoe to the center of the mobile and hang it where guests and family can exchange Christmas kisses.

MATERIALS & EQUIPMENT
balsa wood
shaped cookie cutters or paper for patterns
craft knife • sandpaper • awl
leather or suede ribbon (you could use string or twine)
buttons, feathers, pine cones, and skeleton leaves for decoration
dowel rods (ours were 20 in/50 cm long)
wire
needle • cotton thread • scissors
pencil • double-sided tape • glue

1 Pencil a star and a heart shape onto balsa wood. We drew around cookie cutters, but you could make paper patterns (see page 109) or draw on the wood if your hand is steady. Carefully cut out several stars and hearts with a craft knife.

2 Smooth the edges of the balsa shapes with fine sandpaper. Using an awl, make a hole at the top of each piece big enough to thread a ribbon through. Glue a button in the centers of the shapes.

3 Thread ribbon through each balsa shape and knot or stitch in place. At the free end of each ribbon, stitch a loop to slide over the dowel. Stick or stitch feathers, pine cones, and skeleton leaves onto different lengths of ribbon.

4 Wire the dowels into a cross. Cover wire with leather binding, leaving long ends to hang the mobile. Thread ribboned items onto the dowel, distributing the weight evenly. A button on the end of each dowel will stop things from sliding off.

festive winter mobile 37

Gift wrap and cards

All children love to receive presents, but as we get older, we find ever greater pleasure in giving them, too. We wrap gifts to give others the thrill of opening them, so gorgeous paper, tags, and trims are an important part of the fun, both for the giver and recipient. And, while presents have to wait until Christmas Day, cards give their pleasure in the days before it. Basic techniques and materials are all you need to produce them at home, so your seasonal message is uniquely personal.

LEFT A French paper candy bag was the starting point for this pretty wrapping. The top was rolled down, two holes punched in it, and gold ribbon was threaded through.

wrapping

Wrapping Christmas presents is a ritual you either love or loathe. For one thing, it takes far longer than you'd think, as anyone who's left it all until Christmas Eve can tell you. However, the results bring great pleasure to loved ones, so start at least a week before, and make it fun by using gorgeous papers and trims.

Every mall sells a huge array of wrapping paper, but there are less run-of-the-mill designs available, too, in gift stores, good stationers, and the like. Handmade papers, particularly Japanese ones, often have unusual, textured finishes, while cellophane

LEFT Gift boxes are useful for small items or to disguise the shape of something. Here, paper ribbon curled by pulling across a scissor blade tops a gold star-shaped box.

BOTTOM LEFT A lace doily and vintage tassel make this paper-covered box pretty enough to be a keepsake after Christmas.

BELOW Presents wait beneath the tree, all wrapped in elegant white, gold, and silver and tied with an assortment of ribbons. Fabric roses and silver-sprayed holly leaves replace gift tags.

TOP RIGHT This chic box, tied with a show-stopping red and white polka-dot bow, hints at something luxurious within.

CENTER RIGHT This stylish wrapping has been prepared with a man in mind. The bold red and white paper and restrained black velvet ribbon are festive without being fussy.

BOTTOM RIGHT An opulent red tassel gives a flourish to this gift, wrapped in hand-printed paper.

gives a professional, glossy look and can also be used to overlay other papers (as can thick tracing paper). Don't neglect cost-effective basics such as tissue paper, but try new approaches, such as wrapping gifts in layers of contrasting colors; or using plain white tissue, then adding color interest with ribbon. Ordinary brown parcel paper can be customized by stamping or stenciling it (gold paint looks particularly good), or you can photocopy images onto sheets of plain paper.

OPPOSITE, TOP TO BOTTOM
Hole-punched folded paper,
threaded with white cord,
makes a minimalist trim.

Acting as tag and additional
present, a silver Christmas tree
decoration adds sparkle to this
simple white linen sachet.

These two parcels have been
topped with party poppers
and mini-lights to get their
recipients into the festive spirit.

Conjuring up the magic
of a white Christmas, this
present has been finished
with a feathery snowflake.

LEFT Vintage rhinestone
jewelry, which can be found
inexpensively in secondhand
stores, gives these parcels
glamorous, retro sparkle.

ABOVE Gift wrappings need
not be complicated to look
stunning; here, a scattering
of foil stars and two bands of
silver cord make the difference.

TOP RIGHT Making your own
wrapping paper can be cost-
effective and fun. This image
has been photocopied and
enlarged from an old postcard.

ABOVE RIGHT A flamboyant
trim of feathers and shiny
balls on silver-flecked paper
should put smiles on faces
on Christmas morning.

Handmade papers often have unusual, textured finishes, while cellophane gives a professional, glossy look and can be used to overlay other papers.

Tissue paper is inexpensive and looks great in generous quantities. Here, several sheets have been combined with clear cellophane and used to swathe a pot of heather.

Finishing a present with pretty trims makes all the difference. Ribbon can be tied in large, opulent bows (the wire-edged sort is useful for this, since it holds its shape), and narrow or sheer ribbons can be layered over wide ones. Scour notions counters and craft stores for decorative edgings, braid, cord, fabric or paper flowers, feathers, beaded motifs, feather butterflies, or even quirky buttons to finish your parcels with. Dried seed or flowerheads, fresh or skeleton leaves, pine cones, and berries can all be used, perhaps sprayed festive gold or silver. Christmas decorations—shiny balls, bells, miniature crackers, sparkly stars—are also great additions to parcels and, of course, become an extra gift for the lucky recipient.

ABOVE LEFT This parcel has been given an intriguingly old-fashioned treatment with thick, parchment-colored paper, tape, and sealing wax.

ABOVE CENTER To wrap a cylindrical present neatly, use tissue or crepe, carefully pleated at each end. Trim excess paper before you start.

ABOVE RIGHT To make an envelope, open an existing one to use as a template, scaling it up or down. For best results, use heavyweight paper.

TOP RIGHT Have fun wrapping a conventional gift in an unconventional way. This graphic paper with funky bobble tie hides a bottle of fine wine.

Coordinating tags and paper—
here in a bold, modern abstract
design—gives a pleasingly
professional look to presents.

Special enough to be a gift
itself, this tag incorporates a
sprig of mistletoe made from
pearly beads and gold-sprayed
leaves. You could also finish
a tag with artificial or beaded
berries, sequined butterflies,
or any small, sparkly accessory.

Punched-out shapes are
simple but effective. You could
try it freehand with a craft knife,
though craft suppliers sell
decorative hole punchers to
make the job easier.

A gold-sprayed leaf enhances
this paper tag. You could use
sprayed seed heads, dried
flowers, or nuts in a similar
way. Simple motifs can also be
stamped or stenciled on tags.

This simple star was cut
from thin card stock onto
which sheet music had been
photocopied. You could copy
photographs of Christmas
scenes, or pictures of your
own house and garden to give
presents a personal touch.

CENTER Old documents in
elegant copperplate or italic
can be photocopied and made
into unusual tags or gift wrap
(though check they're from
a copyright-free source first).

gift tags

Labeling presents in unusual ways is an enjoyable challenge, and children can help with many of the most attractive decorative techniques. They can make gingerbread stars or hearts (making a hole before baking), then ice names or initials on them and thread ribbon through. Simple printing can be done with potatoes or by cutting out a motif from cardboard, gluing it to another piece, and attaching a cork to the back as a handle. Use metallic spray paint with stencils, or spray over real leaves or paper doilies. Customize plain tags (luggage labels are ideal) by adding motifs cut from felt or colored card stock. Glue on snowflakes (fold squares of paper or tissue in half to make a triangle, fold in half twice more, then cut away at the sides and open out). Likewise, adorn plain tags with such things as ribbon bows, artificial berries, tiny baubles, sequins, paper roses, or beads.

ABOVE This paper dove looks impressive but isn't hard to make. The body shape is highly simplified, and the wings are just a sheet of pleated paper.

FAR LEFT These hearts were cut from self-hardening clay with cookie cutters. Push buttons in before the clay sets.

PROJECT 5
embossed leaf gift tag

This is a stylish way to dress up a present. Although it's Christmassy, don't use holly—the prickles will tear the embossing sheet. Choose thick, evergreen leaves of a good size such as skimmia, bay, laurel, pittosporum, or some varieties of ivy. You could make changes by using different combinations of ribbon: perhaps silver, gold, and white; purple and ruby red; or red and white. For the best result, use narrow ribbons rather than wide ones and carry on the color theme with your beaded initial. Another simple embossing technique can be done with paper. Draw a shape onto thin card stock and cut it out. Place paper over the card and carefully rub over the shape with the back of a teaspoon.

MATERIALS & EQUIPMENT
gift box
ribbon
double-sided tape
lightweight aluminum art embossing sheets
leaves • sequins
small beads for making initial and larger beads
wire
needle • cotton thread
scissors

1 Turn the lid of your box upside down. Stick the ends of two lengths of ribbon to the interior of the box lid with double-sided tape. This should form a cross on the front of the box (for best results, mark the mid-point of each side first).

2 Place a piece of art foil over a leaf and rub hard. The leaf shape will appear through the foil. Cut the shapes out with scissors and stitch them onto ribbon. Hide the stitches with beads. Stitch sequins onto the ribbon ends for sparkle.

3 Thread beads onto a long piece of wire and make a small loop at the end to stop the beads from sliding off. Bend the beaded wire into the recipient's initial and finish with another small loop to keep the beads in place.

4 Thread all the ribbons through the center of your cross in the middle of your parcel, tying each one on with a simple knot. Finish by tying the initial to a ribbon end and tying a bow in the middle of the ribbons to hide the knots.

ABOVE LEFT This card features a potato-print tree (a holly-leaf print can just be seen behind it). A scattering of glitter and a silver stick-on star add seasonal sparkle.

ABOVE RIGHT For these cards, origami paper has been cut into simple shapes and mounted on plain card.

CENTER LEFT For the simplest of homemade cards, a square of decorative Chinese paper has been stuck onto plain card.

CENTER RIGHT Watercolor paper was used for this card. Stars, cut from leftover wrapping, were stuck down the middle, with star-shaped stickers added to the centers.

making cards

Making cards is popular with children, and homespun greetings are particularly appreciated by grandparents and other family members. Unless you're very artistic, keep things simple for the best results. Collage is fun, creating seasonal motifs—snowmen, stockings, trees, stars, crowns, and so on—from materials such as candy wrappers, spare wrapping paper, scraps of fabric, felt, and colored card stock. Add glitter, sequins, buttons, beads, paint-sprayed dried leaves, or anything else that adds texture and sparkle. Think ahead and keep some of the cards you're sent, bringing them out the following

ABOVE LEFT If you're trying collage, keep shapes simple and stylized so that fussy details don't detract from the impact of papers and fabrics in bold colors and patterns.

ABOVE CENTER The simplest of shapes and color combinations (here, white and gold) produces stylish results.

ABOVE RIGHT For this simple but clever cut-out card, fold a piece of card stock in half, open it, then cut a silhouette on one side with a craft knife. Fold it back for a 3-D effect.

LEFT Felt can often be bought in multicolored bulk packs from craft suppliers. It's a worthwhile investment at the start of the season, as it can be used for so many projects.

LEFT This understated brown-paper tree has been given seasonal sparkle with a rhinestone and a touch of gold on the edge of the card.

CENTER LEFT These rustic cards were made by sticking twig "trees" to watercolor paper. The recipients' names are included in the form of handwritten tags.

BOTTOM LEFT Relatives will appreciate a card made with an old family photograph, finished here with gold braid and frayed old-gold ribbon.

BELOW Findings from thrift stores and antique emporiums can be turned into distinctive cards. Here, buttons, crystals, and rhinestone buckles embellish plain cream cards.

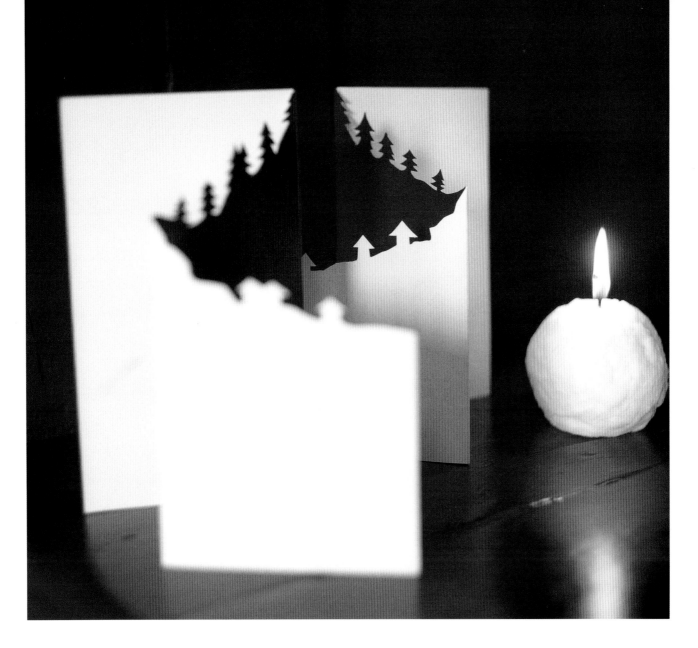

Cut out snowflakes from white paper or tissue, then mount them on cards in a contrasting color such as dark green, red, or midnight blue.

Christmas for children to cut up. Cut out snowflakes from white paper or tissue (see page 47), then mount them on cards in a contrasting color such as dark green, red, or midnight blue. Alternatively, cut shapes out of the front of a plain card and glue contrasting paper or tissue behind to give a stained-glass effect. If you need to mass-produce cards, rubber stamps or stencils are very useful and look stylish used with metallic paint or spray.

ABOVE To make these delightful snowy vignettes, fold thick white card stock in three. Glue colored paper on the middle section, then use a craft knife to cut out the shapes of trees and log cabins.

origami bird Christmas card

While not traditionally Christmassy, patterned Japanese origami paper is a pretty choice for these cheerful little robins. If you can't get hold of origami paper, use good-quality wrapping paper with a small floral pattern. Sewing on card stock may seem unlikely, but it's easy and highly effective. If you want to make a number of cards and have a sewing machine, use this for speed. Try metallic thread and setting the machine on zigzag stitch to create more abstract patterns. Another simple card-making technique is to punch holes around the edge and thread ribbon or cord in and out to make a border. A festive motif can be cut from paper or card and stuck in the middle.

MATERIALS & EQUIPMENT
craft paper (or ready-cut cards) and envelopes
carpenter's square • craft knife
origami paper (you can buy this in squares or rolls)
embroidery thread
leaves • gold spray paint
rhinestone "jewels" • mirror disks
feather
scissors • needle
PVA glue • double-sided tape

1 Cut out card stock to fit your envelopes using a square and craft knife, scoring the center fold. Make a bird shape template (see page 110) and draw around it on the back of the origami paper. Cut out a bird and several leaf shapes.

2 Stitch a simple branch design onto the card using running stitch and a contrasting color of embroidery thread. Spray a selection of leaves gold. Always use spray paint in a well-ventilated area.

3 Use PVA glue to stick the origami-paper bird to the front of the card and give it a rhinestone eye. Complete your design by adding small mirror disks, origami-paper leaves, gold-sprayed leaves, and finally a feather to make the bird's wing.

4 To cover the stitching on the inside of the card, cut out backing from origami paper using a square and craft knife. Attach this using double-sided tape. To complete, add a cut-out star and rhinestone jewel to the envelope.

FAR RIGHT The hall is a great place for displaying cards, creating an immediate sense of welcome. Here, cards have been sandwiched around lengths of ribbon and their edges glued together. The ends of the ribbon are tucked under the stair carpet and secured with tape.

ABOVE RIGHT Many stores sell packs of cord and miniature clothespins for creating a festive clothesline of cards.

BELOW For an instant display, what could be easier than placing cards on a mantelpiece or windowsill? To heighten their decorative impact, group them by color and size.

LEFT If you don't want to clutter surfaces with cards, open them and slip the backs between books on a shelf.

displaying cards

Make the most of the cards you receive, because they're quick and easy to decorate with. There's nothing wrong with the traditional approach of displaying them on open shelves, mantelpieces, and windowsills, but increase their impact by grouping the cards according to size and color or arranging baubles, fairy lights, or greenery among them. If you don't want cards littering surfaces, tuck them between books, into mirror frames, or behind pictures. Make a card "tree" by putting several branches in a large vase or flowerpot, punching holes in the top of your cards, threading through pretty ribbon, and tying them on. Cards can also be attached to long lengths of wide ribbon and then hung on door backs, walls, or stairs.

Twig mesh, from florists, can
be attached to a door or wall
for cards to be hung from.
Colorful narrow ribbon and
tiny balls add to the display.

Tree decorations

If one thing embodies Christmas, it's the tree, whether
your choice is a six-foot Norwegian spruce or an
arrangement of white-sprayed branches. Bringing out
the box of treasured ornaments collected over the years
is a cherished ritual for many. Although an array of highly
ornate purchased decorations creates a spectacular
effect on the tree, there's much to be said for simpler,
homemade versions, too, particularly those which every
member of the family can get involved in making.

The joy of Christmas decorations is that they all somehow work together, so if you've amassed an eclectic collection just put them all up and enjoy!

To make a paper star, pleat a rectangle of paper, fold in half and secure at the center with fine wire. Cut deep points in the edges of the pleats. Fan into a star and tape the ends.

balls and baubles

The modern Christmas tree as we know it dates to the nineteenth century, when Prince Albert introduced to Britain the German practice of decorating a tree with candles, wooden toys, and glass ornaments. Purists consider a real tree the only type worth having, but you can also buy very realistic artificial ones. To help a real tree last, water it regularly and stand it away from heat. For something more original, consider a twig tree (left natural or sprayed), or even a metal one.

Getting out the tree decorations is one of the most magical of Christmas moments and putting them on (starting with lights) is often a family effort. Theming

ABOVE LEFT Vintage finds can, with a little imagination, become decorations. Here, a rhinestone and opaline earring sparkles against a tree's dark branches.

ABOVE CENTER This glamorous homemade tassel was concocted from metallic fringed braid, rhinestones, and a loop of fine wire.

ABOVE RIGHT Victorian decorations inspired this tree, which is laden with lavender hearts, feather birds, faux flowers, and real candles.

TOP RIGHT Star-shaped spice cookies are suspended from a tree by narrow gingham ribbon. Make holes in cookies with a skewer before baking.

ornaments by color or style looks very effective (see pages 22–29). However, the joy of Christmas decorations is that they all somehow work together, so if you've lovingly amassed an eclectic collection over the years just put them all up together and enjoy!

Decorations are big business and available from specialized companies all year round, but making your own ornaments is fun and surprisingly easy. A good way to start is by customizing purchased balls (see page 64).

ABOVE LEFT Care for your decorations and they'll last for decades. Wrap in tissue and store in boxes with cardboard dividers, or in egg boxes.

LEFT India is a great source of decorative ornaments. This stuffed-cloth elephant is smothered in brightly colored embroidery and braid.

ABOVE Perfect for a homespun Christmas, gingerbread or spiced cookies can be cut into seasonal shapes such as these jolly snowmen and hung from the tree with pretty ribbon.

ABOVE Decorations made from honeycombed tissue paper, such as these pretty fruits, look exquisite but are delicate, so they need gentle handling if they're to survive.

ABOVE LEFT If you're after a modern but not minimalist look, try combining plain glass and striped balls in a kaleidoscope of zingy colors.

LEFT Make stained-glass cookies by cutting circles out of cookies before cooking and placing hard candy in the hole, then baking as normal.

BELOW LEFT If you're decorating a tree for your children, load it with colorful wrapped candy, lollipops, and candy canes.

balls and baubles 63

PROJECT 7
beaded baubles

Plain balls, whether clear or colored, glossy or frosted, are easy to transform into unique ornaments using readily available materials. Here cool pinks, blues, and purples have been used in place of traditional red and gold, and tiny sequins, sparkly beads, and delicate flowers produce a sophisticated rather than gaudy effect. Other variations are even simpler to achieve. Use PVA glue to draw swirls, stars, or stripes onto balls, then roll them in glitter spread on a plate. Alternatively, create patterns with tubes of metallic contour paste or glass outliner (from craft suppliers). You could also try finishing off your baubles with feathers, glittery butterflies, small shells, or pine cones (perhaps sprayed with metallic paint), wired beads, or clusters of fake berries.

MATERIALS & EQUIPMENT
plain tree balls
PVA glue
rhinestones and sequins
tweezers (optional)
small glass beads
thin wire
small paper or fabric flowers
ribbon
old brooches, bracelets, and necklaces
needle • cotton thread

1 Place a ball in a cup to hold it upright. Dab small blobs of PVA glue onto the surface in your desired pattern. Let the glue dry slightly or the decorations may slide off. Apply rhinestones or sequins (it may help to use tweezers).

2 To make a hanging loop, thread small glass beads on a short length of doubled cotton thread. Knot one end first to stop the beads from slipping off. Pass the beads through the hoop at the top of the ball. Tie the ends together.

3 Wire the stems of three or more small artificial flowers. Wire them around the metal fixture at the top of the ball; you may be able to poke the stems down through the perforations into the center of the ball itself.

4 Tie a ribbon bow around the top to hide any visible flower stems and wires. Finish off by adding a vintage brooch, pendant, or other jewelry item. Attach it to the ribbon or to the glass-bead loop.

BELOW These Indian baubles, glittering with metallic thread, hark back to medieval designs and would lend an antique air to a traditional scheme.

RIGHT This plain cardboard shape (look for these in craft catalogs) has been simply decorated with silver and gold stars for a handcrafted look.

RIGHT These glass and wire balls, all in silvery shades, show that texture and finish are as ornamental as pattern.

BELOW LEFT AND CENTER For a snow-dusted effect, this real tree was misted with florist's spray and decorated in white, gold, and silver. Pearly shells, glittery fabric butterflies, and metallic glass balls create a fantastical effect.

FAR RIGHT In a homage to Victoriana, charmingly old-fashioned decorations such as feathered birds, satin ribbons, and bead berries nestle in the branches of this tree.

Other simple projects to try are baking shaped gingerbread or cookies to hang up; spraying pine cones gold or silver; covering styrofoam balls (from craft suppliers) with fabric, beads, or sequins; painting ready-cut wooden shapes (also from craft suppliers); cutting out paper snowflakes (see page 47), Christmas trees, or stars; sewing or gluing tiny felt stockings; cutting shapes from salt dough (mix two cups plain flour, one cup salt and water), then baking and painting them; making bows from wire-edged ribbon; or wrapping stock cubes or matchboxes to look like miniature parcels.

RIGHT With its key role in the nativity story, a star is one of the two favorite tree toppers, the other being an angel. Here, a star encrusted with gold sequins strikes a glamorous note. Make your own from gold card and cover with sequins.

FAR RIGHT A gorgeously plump robin surveys this white tree decked temptingly with candy just waiting to be unwrapped.

BELOW This traditional tree, decorated with red and gold ornaments and tiny white crackers, has been finished with a flamboyant bow made from wire-edged ribbon.

tree toppers

Many of us like to crown the tree with a special decoration. Because of their powerful Christmas symbolism, angels (or the secular version, fairies) and stars are traditionally popular. Stars can be cut from thick card stock and spray-painted, covered in sequins or doused in glitter. Try twisting four equal lengths of heavy wire together in the middle to make an eight-pointed frame, then bind tinsel around each arm. Use a star-shaped cookie cutter with salt dough (see page 66) or self-hardening clay, then decorate and varnish the result. A simple angel silhouette can be cut from card, wood, clay, or dough and painted, or try the delightful clothespin version overleaf. However, there's no need to be slavishly traditional. A beaded snowflake, snowman (perhaps made from white wool pompoms), extravagant ribbon bow, or a feather bird might take pride of place. Position a fairy light just below your tree topper to act as a mini-uplighter.

This delightful fairy was modeled from self-hardening clay, with a dress of tulle and tissue paper, and wings, tiara, and corsage made from beads threaded onto fine wire.

PROJECT 8
fairy tree topper

This enchanting creature, with her delicate feather wings, full skirt, earrings, and piled-up hairdo, is based on a wooden clothespin. Clothespins might be humble and practical, but they're also a brilliant craft item. Tracking them down is sometimes tricky, but old-fashioned hardware stores usually stock them, as well as craft suppliers. Once you've made one fairy, you might want to produce a number of them in different pretty outfits to line up on a windowsill or mantelpiece, or suspend from a doorway. You could also make them as presents and delight any little girls in the family by leaving one in their stocking. Try using fabrics for the fairies' clothes such as fine cotton, muslin, silk, or tulle in pale pink, lilac, pistachio, sky blue, and lemon yellow. If fairies seem a little too secular, make an angel tree topper instead by leaving aside the wand, dressing the doll in lacy white fabric, and swapping her star hair accessory for a gold halo.

MATERIALS & EQUIPMENT
delicate fabric for skirt and blouse (see template on page 110)
felt for legs and arms (see templates on page 110)
pencil • black and red pens
wooden clothespin
yarn for hair
two sequin stars • two sequins
assorted ribbons
feathers
match
wire
scissors • double-sided tape • PVA glue

1 Cut out a skirt using a saucer as a guide. Fold the fabric into eighths. Cut scallops around the curved edge and a small hole at the top. Next cut a rectangle with a notch at the top for the blouse, as above. Cut felt legs and arms.

2 Pencil a face onto the head as a guide, then go over lightly with a fine black pen for eyes and red for lips. Brush head with glue and slowly wind yarn around, adding more glue as necessary. Glue a star to the yarn. Add sequins for earrings.

3 Stick your fairy's blouse onto the pin using double-sided tape or PVA glue. Thread the skirt onto the pin; hold skirt in place with thick ribbon attached with double-sided tape. Glue on a small ribbon bow in a contrasting color.

4 Attach arms and legs with double-sided tape and glue on feather "wings." Use ribbon to hide the workings. Cut off the end of a match and glue on a star to make a wand; attach to the inside of one hand. Wire the fairy to your treetop.

Table decorations

The Christmas meal is an eagerly awaited event, and a special table setting will heighten your guests' pleasure in it. You might want to keep things simple, with church candles down the length of the table or a cake stand casually piled with metallic balls; or you might prefer the drama of a centerpiece of frosted fruits and gleaming candelabra. Whether the table setting is grand or low-key, stylish details—beribboned napkins, handwritten name tags—will make your meal one to linger over.

table settings and centerpieces

The Christmas meal is the social focus of the day, so time spent
dressing your table beautifully will never be wasted. Take stock
of your china and glassware first, choosing extras—flowers,
candles, table linen, crackers, napkin rings, and so on—that
work sympathetically with them. Red and green is a tried and
tested color combination, or you could try white with silver; rich
purples and reds; white and red; or rustic neutrals highlighted
with gold. White table linen is a flattering backdrop to any
scheme. However, for such a special occasion, you might want
a decorative runner or cloth, perhaps in shimmering organza

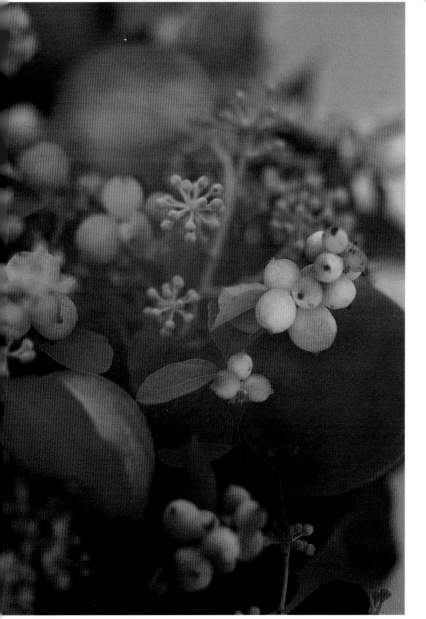

OPPOSITE TOP LEFT Making a dramatic partnership, a dark purple candle sits above clusters of snowberries.

OPPOSITE TOP RIGHT The dark days of winter are the right time for opulent color schemes; here, sumptuous dusky purple with ruby red.

ABOVE LEFT A pot pourri of pine cones, cinnamon sticks, citrus slices, and clove-studded pomanders will scent the air.

ABOVE Fragrant bulbs such as hyacinths (shown here) and narcissi can be forced so that they're in flower at Christmas.

LEFT Shiny red apples, crab apples, rosehips, and berries from shrubs such as snowberry, viburnum, and cotoneaster look spectacular with evergreens.

table settings and centerpieces 75

or beaded silk. You could place baubles at place settings or pile them in dishes, perhaps even lay a string of fairy lights down the center of the table. Finally, a centerpiece creates a visual and conversational focal point, whether it's an arrangement of flowers and candles or, more spectacular still, a dish piled high with frosted fruits (brush them with lightly beaten egg white, then dredge with sugar and leave to dry).

LEFT A tiny galvanized bucket holds variegated foliage. Damp florist's foam and a plastic liner are hidden under white tissue.

BELOW Sugared almonds make a pretty addition to have with coffee and mince pies.

ABOVE RIGHT White, gold, and silver balls in a variety of finishes have been piled into a glass dish to create an easy, instant decorative centerpiece.

RIGHT Fairy lights needn't be restricted to the tree. Thread them through small balls and lay them down the table as an illuminated runner.

LEFT This grand table sets the scene for a feast. Magnificent candelabras with purple candles, purple glassware, a centerpiece of frosted fruits, and extravagant flowers create sophisticated opulence.

rich berry table runner

If you've got a classic plain white tablecloth, adding a decorative runner will give it a makeover for the festive season. If you don't like tablecloths, a runner is a stylish alternative, giving a less formal look than a traditional large cloth. Choose a fabric with a bit of weight so it hangs well and is firm enough to be embroidered easily. A neutral or white background will draw the eye to the pretty detail, but you could use material in a dramatic shade such as damson or raspberry and continue with beads, thread, and ribbon in the same palette, perhaps highlighted with gold.

MATERIALS & EQUIPMENT
fabric to make the runner
embroidery thread
beads (or fake berries)
contrasting fabric to make leaves (see templates on page 111)
selection of ribbons
pins • needle • cotton thread • scissors

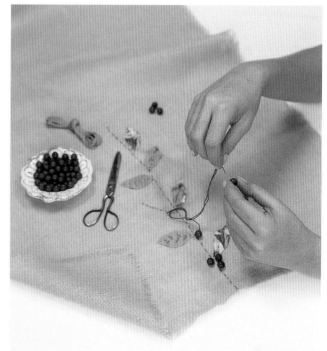

1 Cut a length of fabric to match your table size, making it long enough so the embroidery will hang down off the ends of the table. We used linen, which is heavy enough to sit well. The edges were fringed to complete the look.

2 Find the center point at each end of the fabric. Using embroidery thread, create a "stem" in running stitch. Carry the stem onto the tabletop, but leave the central area free for serving dishes. Stitch on bead "berries" and fabric leaves.

3 Cut lengths of ribbon to make a decorative edging. We used ribbons of varying width, color, and texture to add interest. Pin the ribbons on the runner and secure with small stitches. The outer ribbon will stop the fabric from fraying too far.

4 Make four ribbon bows in a matching or contrasting ribbon to your edging, and add one to each corner. Of course, you don't have to stop there; you can add as much or as little decoration to this runner as you like.

Breadsticks grouped in
glasses bear guests' names.

These homemade crackers
double as place cards.

Embroidered felt stars were
sewn onto these place cards.

ABOVE RIGHT This place card
has been threaded onto raffia
and decorated with crab
apples to act as a napkin ring.

place cards

Christmas is a time when we make time for formal details that we
otherwise would not. Decorative place cards are an attractive touch
and can be used to reinforce your table setting's color scheme
and style. All the techniques used to make gift tags (see pages
46–49) can be applied here, so you could make place cards at
the same time as doing your wrapping. If you don't feel that your
calligraphic skills are up to hand-writing your cards, check out the
fonts on your computer and print the names instead.

ABOVE These angel's wings were cut from sheets of craft metal and attached to thin wire. The wire was then threaded through the top of each folded place card.

RIGHT Simple but stylish, an ordinary luggage label has been elegantly inscribed with the diner's name and threaded onto gleaming ribbon to tie up a knife and fork.

Look for ribbons in all widths and colors, from sheer to satin, as well as tassels, braid, lace, and cord, plus buttons and beads to thread on.

LEFT Claret ribbon, purple foliage, and glowing red berries dress up a white napkin and complement ruby-red glasses.

BELOW LEFT Cheerful tartan ribbon and scarlet poppy anemones update traditional seasonal red and green.

BOTTOM LEFT These delightfully rustic napkin rings were fashioned from thin, flexible birch twigs, sprigs of evergreen foliage, and small clusters of snowberries. Grouped in a wire basket with pine cones and foliage, they also make an attractive display.

BELOW Small bronze balls, tied onto green-gold ribbon, strike a tastefully opulent note.

RIGHT A ring of corrugated paper holds this napkin tightly so that the ends fan out. A tree decoration of wire and beads reinforces the modern look.

napkin rings

You may not use napkin rings every day, but if there's ever a time to use them, it's Christmas. Notions departments are a good source of all manner of items that can be used to cinch napkins. Look for ribbons in all widths and colors, from sheer to satin, as well as tassels, braid, lace, and cord, plus buttons and beads to thread on for embellishment. You could also add feathers, real or fabric flowers, small Christmas decorations, glittery butterflies, seasonal foliage, nuts, or fruit.

ABOVE, CLOCKWISE FROM TOP LEFT Sequined braid, with a white feather tucked under, secures damask napkins.

This napkin tie is pompom braid, sold to edge cushions.

Sequined braid, pleated ribbon, and cord, all in silvers and grays, tie identical napkins.

Glamorous beaded tassels add a note of luxury.

PROJECT 10
flower napkin ring and brooch

These gorgeous fabric flowers are dual-purpose, serving to brighten your Christmas table and, for female guests, become a keepsake. Layering shapes of increasing size to make a 3-D flower is a simple but effective technique. Cotton fabric, printed or plain, is ideal for this project, since it may be difficult to get a needle through layers of heavier fabric. Using different but toning colors for each layer looks good, and you could try using successively darker shades toward the center, or vice versa. Soft, slightly faded colors such as dusty pinks and muted reds will give a vintage feel to the flowers, or you could use more dramatic shades—think of dark, velvety roses for inspiration—and extra sequins for really sumptuous blooms.

MATERIALS & EQUIPMENT
tracing paper for templates
variety of fabrics
buttons, sequins, and beads
rhinestones
ribbon
brooch back
pins • needle • cotton thread
scissors • glue

1 Make paper templates of a flower shape in five increasing sizes (see page 111). Pin onto fabric and cut out the five shapes for each flower you need. We used different fabrics for each layer. Also cut out two leaf shapes for each flower.

2 Stack the flower pieces with the largest at the bottom and smallest on top. Keep in place with a few stitches. Place a button on top, stitching through all the layers. Thread beads and sequins through, too. Glue on rhinestones to add sparkle.

3 Stitch a fabric leaf onto each end of a length of narrow ribbon, adding sequins or sequin shapes for extra glitter. Cut a narrow oval hole in the center of one leaf, to pass the other leaf through when on the napkin.

4 Stitch a brooch back onto the reverse of your flower and pass the ribbon through to complete the napkin ring. Fold napkins flat to display the flower well. After the meal, remove the ribbon and your guests have a flower brooch.

flower napkin ring and brooch 85

Wreaths and garlands

Christmas is a time of hospitality, when we throw open our doors to friends and family with parties and gatherings. A wreath on the front door—whether made of evergreen boughs, flowers and berries, or woven twigs doused in glitter and twinkling with fairy lights—signals the start of the festive season, suggesting that a warm welcome will be found within. Inside the house, garlands continue the celebratory mood, from simple paper chains to flamboyant swags of greenery or sparkling silver.

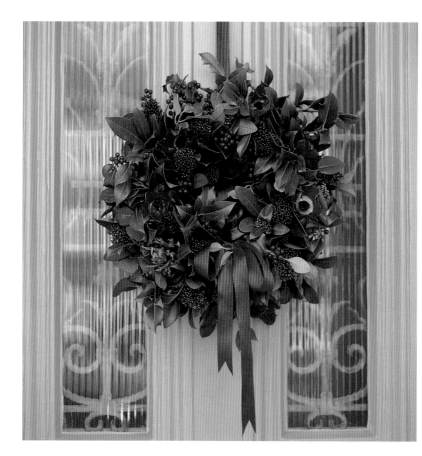

wreaths

A front door displaying a beribboned wreath suggests festive cheer to visitors. However, the materials used for an outdoor wreath must be able to withstand the elements; position more delicate creations inside, on a mantelpiece, a picture hook on a wall, or an internal door. If you want to make a wreath from scratch, make a circle from strong wire or by twisting pliable twigs together, then use florist's wire to attach real or artificial leaves, berries, flowers, nuts, or fruit. For a short cut, moss and foam circles can be bought from florists; they are ready to decorate in the same way. Even easier, a ready-made wreath of twigs (which you could spray-paint) or artificial pine can be redecorated differently each year, since it's just a question of adding ribbons, baubles, lights, or any other decorations that take your fancy.

LEFT The traditional place for a wreath is the front door. Here, scarlet ribbon secures a circle of bay, viburnum, and holly leaves (plus their berries), and jewel-bright anemones.

ABOVE This purchased wreath of artificial berries has been enlivened by adding more artificial berries, this time in a brighter red, and an elegant red velvet streamer. Invisible fishing line was then attached to the wreath, taken over the top of the door and looped over a hook on the back.

RIGHT A circle of birch twigs has been given a bold, modern look by being painted red and dipped in glitter. Tiny fairy lights were then threaded through from behind.

OPPOSITE TOP RIGHT For rustic with a hint of glitz, gold-headed pins stud a wreath of crab apples.

ABOVE RIGHT Sculpted and sliced citrus fruits such as the ones used to make this fragrant wreath can be dried in an ultra-low warming oven.

RIGHT These glycerined beech leaves (from florists) have been crafted into a beautifully natural wreath for a refreshing change from traditional evergreens.

A ready-made wreath of twigs or artificial pine can be redecorated differently each year.

ABOVE The basis of this charming country wreath was a thin wire frame. Variegated ivy and snowberry branches were attached to it with florist's wire. All sorts of other plant material could be wired onto a frame in the same way, from dried hops and seed heads to evergreens such as skimmia, euonymus, pine, and heathers, and flowers such as roses.

ABOVE RIGHT Old letters in an elegant hand were photocopied onto heavy paper to make this simple wreath, based on a wire frame. The paper was cut into oak-leaf shapes and some were sprayed gold. Gilded rosehips were also wired on at intervals around the wreath.

RIGHT For this icy wreath, skeleton leaves and dried seed heads (poppies and love-in-a-mist are good choices) were wired onto a ready-made twig wreath. Dipped in plaster of Paris, the wreath takes on a dramatic, sculptural quality.

ABOVE AND ABOVE LEFT
This small, spidery wire wreath,
decorated with tiny beads,
some transparent, some white,
hooks neatly over the key on
a cupboard door.

ABOVE CENTER Long-
stemmed dried flowers were
looped into a circle and held
with wire to make this simple
wreath. Dried oak leaves were
then added, and the whole
wreath sprayed gold.

LEFT This clever snowflake
is based on a frame of six
ordinary bamboo stakes.
When pine branches are wired
on, their leaves produce a
perfect snowflake pattern.

RIGHT If you have guests for Christmas, it's fun to extend the decorations to their room. This paper Santa garland, strung from the headboard, gives instant cheer.

BELOW RIGHT Mini mittens (which could be knitted or made from felt) are a delightful alternative to paper chains.

FAR RIGHT This wood-burning stove has been given a festive facelift with giant balls and branches of leylandii.

BELOW A splendid traditional display of greenery, berries, and balls makes a grand show.

garlands

Great swags of greenery, fruit, and berries create a dramatic and satisfyingly traditional decorative statement, particularly when adorning a mantelpiece or staircase. Making a garland from fresh plant material is quite a task, but unadorned fresh and artificial garlands are readily available, and you can customize them with ribbons, baubles, artificial berries, flowers, and so on. If you want something different, consider a wintry white garland, hung with glass "icicles" or beaded snowflakes. Nor do all garlands need to be grand—after all, paper chains are an essential part of the festivities for many children. Instead of precut gummed strips, make links from wide ribbon, or hang card stars sprinkled with glitter from string or fishing line. Alternatively, glue pieces of wrapping paper back to back, then cut into strips to make into chains.

In a conscious departure from traditional greenery, this magical, sparkling garland is composed of beaded wire, feather butterflies, and glittery metallic balls. It looks magnificent against the backdrop of a white staircase.

PROJECT 11
scented wreath

Decorating with evergreens goes back to pre-Christian times, when trees and plants that retained their leaves through the darkest days of the year represented the hope of the return of spring. Wreaths can decorate doors inside or out, chair backs, or mantelpieces. Here, the gray-green, aromatic leaves of eucalyptus make a striking change from the usual forest-green winter foliage. Seasonal sparkle is introduced in the form of sequins and glass droplets and beads. If you can't find eucalyptus, you could try senecio, variegated ivy, blue-green conifer, or even dried hydrangea heads.

MATERIALS & EQUIPMENT
moss
14-inch (35-cm) diameter wire wreath frame
wire
eucalyptus branches and pods
assorted crystals and large sequins
assorted ribbons
chandelier droplets

1   Dampen the moss. Use it to cover the wreath frame, wiring in place where necessary. If the moss is very densely packed and securely tucked into the framework, you may not need to wire it in place.

2   Cut the eucalyptus into sections about 12 in (30 cm) long. Wire together into bunches of three stems each. Do the same with the pods. Wire branch and pod bunches onto the wreath, overlapping sections slightly to cover the moss.

3   Thread crystals (we used five) on a length of wire to make a flower. Twist the wire to secure. Add large sequins and twist again to hold them in place. Wire the crystal flowers on the wreath at regular intervals. Tuck in loose ends.

4   Tie a length of wide ribbon onto the top of the wreath and make a bow, leaving generous ends. Tie the chandelier droplets from lengths of ribbon at the bottom of the wreath. Use different lengths and colors of ribbon.

Candles

The gentle glow of candlelight creates an atmosphere like nothing else and looks magical in the darkness of midwinter. Most of us don't risk naked flames on the tree, but there are many other ways to use candles around the home—creating a warm welcome in jelly-jar holders on a windowsill, flickering on a mantelpiece, or set among flowers and shiny balls for a striking table centerpiece. From tall pillar candles to votives, candles are an easy and inexpensive way to evoke the spirit of Christmas.

CLOCKWISE FROM RIGHT Placing candles in front of a reflective surface, whether a mirror or, as here, a glass brick wall, heightens their impact. These chunky candles and white pebbles create a simple, but dramatic, display.

This quirky handmade paper bowl is thin enough for the glow of a candle to be seen through it.

These glass jars, trimmed with garden ivy, make a charmingly homey display on a windowsill.

BELOW A mantelpiece is a great place for creating a focal point. Here, an eclectic group of candles and holders makes a pretty and informal display.

room displays

Candlelight is mellow and flattering to anything that it touches. It looks dramatic in an interior, casting strange shadows and creating an atmosphere of times past. In addition, scented candles mean that we can conjure up the spicy aromas of the season at the strike of a match. Grouping candles on a wide shelf, windowsill, or mantelpiece makes good safety sense and creates an impact. Try interspersing them with baubles, white pebbles, greenery, or pine cones; or arranging a collection of candles and small vases holding deep-red roses. Alternatively, use votives en masse, surrounded by glass nuggets. If you have an empty fireplace, fill it with altar candles in a variety of heights. Finally, don't forget your outside space: what could be more inviting for guests than a path illuminated by candles in terra cotta pots or metal lanterns?

Beaded snowflakes (sold as tree decorations) cast delicate shadows along the length of this mantelpiece, which has been lit by a collection of votives, some of them in small galvanized pots.

table displays

Candles create a sense of occasion and conviviality, so are an indispensable part of the festive table. Maximize their twinkle with reflective elements such as sparkling glass or polished metal. For safety, place candles in the center of the table or down its length. Chunky pillar versions and votives look good, or anchor tapers in a bowl using sand, pebbles, or balls. A glass bowl filled with water, floating candles, and flowers makes a spectacular centerpiece.

LEFT This rustic table features a bough of crab apples flanked by thick candles. The napkin rings are made from birch twigs and snowberries.

ABOVE This red, green, and gold setting reeks of the exotic. Red candles anchored in red sand sit in wineglasses at each place setting.

OPPOSITE TOP LEFT Candles reinforce the opulence of this table setting, held in tree candle clips around the edge of a circular mirror, on which sit gold and bronze balls.

OPPOSITE CENTER LEFT An arrangement of bright red berries is complemented by a glowing red candle at its center.

ABOVE LEFT Making this glowing centerpiece is simplicity itself: sit short candles on a china cake stand and add tiny bronze balls.

ABOVE RIGHT These small glasses are wrapped in metallic crepe paper. You could also use glass jars or votive holders.

LEFT Chunky candles sit on a bronze and burgundy sari-fabric table runner, interspersed with distressed-gold balls.

ABOVE Decorative paper bags like these can be bought from candle suppliers, or you could cut out your own design. Votive candles anchored in sand sit at the bottom of the bags.

CENTER Customize a plain glass candle holder with a sash of ribbon and short length of silken cord.

candle holders

If you have a stylish candelabra, now's the time to use it, perhaps dressed up with ivy and clusters of berries. If you don't, scour the house for containers to turn into candle holders. Clean jelly, yogurt, or baby food jars can be pressed into service, spruced up with ribbon or ivy around their rims. Place candles inside old tea or coffee cups, galvanized or terra cotta pots, or pretty shells. Inexpensive metal lanterns look wonderful ranged along a mantelpiece or windowsill. Even simpler, glue metallic braid around the outside of ordinary votives for an instant makeover.

OPPOSITE BELOW, FROM LEFT
A votive sits in an orange holder. Scoop a hole in the top and stud the rim with cloves.

Decorative cinnamon sticks can be bought from florists. Glued around a candle holder, they will exude their aroma as the candle burns.

A candle shaped like a lotus flower sits in a glass goblet, with bear grass coiled inside for added impact.

ABOVE Paper doilies have been wrapped around these glass votive holders. Try the same idea with tracing paper, colored cellophane, or tissue.

LEFT The holes in these small ceramic beakers will create an enchanting effect as dusk falls and the candles are lit.

PROJECT 12
lace votives

These patterned glass votive holders produce a very pretty effect when all the candles are lit. It's possible to buy new tumblers very cheaply, but you could also look for them in thrift stores. If you want to employ the votives in a formal display—perhaps running along a mantelpiece or down the center of a table—choose glasses in one size. For a more informal arrangement, use glasses of different thicknesses and heights. If you're going to roll the glasses in glitter instead of spray-painting them, use glitter with very fine particles (you may have to buy it from a craft supplier) or the pattern won't be reproduced accurately. You can also customize plain glasses very simply with paper and fabric, stuck on with adhesive spray. Cover the outside with tracing paper to produce a frosted effect, or try colored tissue paper, white or gold doilies, metallic crepe paper, or wide organza ribbon. To protect the surface the candles will sit on, you could also decorate coasters or a tray to match.

MATERIALS & EQUIPMENT
glasses of different sizes
lace
repositionable adhesive spray
newspaper
spray paint
glitter or silver leaf and soft brush (optional)
ribbon
double-sided tape
votive candles
scissors

1 Select glasses for your display. You might want to try out groupings before you begin decorating the glasses. Wrap lace around each glass and cut it to size with scissors. You should end up with a rectangle of lace for each glass.

2 Spray a lace rectangle with repositionable adhesive and smooth it onto the outside of its glass. Do this in a well-ventilated area and place newspaper under the glass to protect your work surface.

3 Spray paint evenly onto the glass through the lace. Build up coverage slowly. When the paint is dry, peel lace off slowly to reveal the pattern. Or, spray adhesive through the lace. Peel off and roll in glitter or silver leaf. Brush gently with a soft brush.

4 Cut lengths of ribbon to wrap around each glass and make matching ribbon bows. Stick both onto the glasses with double-sided tape. Add votives, and remember that the glasses will become hot when the candles are lit.

sources

**CHRISTMAS SHOPS/
DECORATIONS**

ALWAYS CHRISTMAS
3033 West Parker
Plano, TX 75023
877-596-7695
www.alwayschristmas
  texas.com
*North Texas' largest
year-round Christmas
store carries ornaments
and decorations, as well
as trees, lights, and
collectibles.*

BED BATH & BEYOND
Locations nationwide
Call 800-462-3966 or visit
www.bedbathandbeyond.com
for details of your nearest
store.
*Candles, tableware,
decorations, and novelty
items for the holidays.*

CARLTON CARDS
Locations nationwide.
Call 800-679-8343 or visit
www.carltoncards.com for
details of your nearest store.
*Cards, ornaments,
decorations, collectibles,
heirloom ornaments, and
more for the holidays.*

THE CHRISTMAS SHOP
307 Bull Street
Savannah, GA 31404
800-569-0330
www.the-christmas-shop.com
*Hard-to-find Christmas
ornaments, decorations,
and collectibles.*

CRATE AND BARREL
Locations nationwide
Call 800-967-6696 or visit
www.crateandbarrel.com for
details of your nearest store.
*Stylish tableware, table
linen, and candles.*

DILLARD'S
Locations nationwide.
Visit dillards.com for details
of your nearest store.
*A selection of gifts and
decorations for the holidays.*

HALLMARK
Locations nationwide
Visit www.hallmark.com for
details of your nearest store.
*Large stock of Christmas
and greeting cards, gift
wrap, novelty items,
ornaments, and more.*

OUTER BANKS
CHRISTMAS SHOP
621 South US 64
Manteo, NC 27954
800-470-2838
www.outerbanks
  christmas.com
*Gifts, music boxes, jewelry,
toys, candles, stationery,
and more.*

RESTORATION HARDWARE
Locations nationwide.
Call 800-762-1005 or visit
www.restorationhardware.
com for details of your
nearest store
*Ornaments and vintage-style
holiday gifts.*

TARGET
Locations nationwide.
Visit target.com for details
of your nearest store.
*A large selection of cards,
decorations, food, and more
for the holidays.*

THE UNION SQUARE
HOLIDAY MARKET
14th Street between
Broadway and University
Place
New York, NY
*Each year, Union Square
features a Holiday Bazaar
with handmade goods, toys,
crafts, and ornaments.*

CRAFT SUPPLIERS

A.C. MOORE
Locations throughout
eastern United States.
Visit acmoore.com for details
of your nearest store.
*A wide selection of
art and craft materials.*

HOBBY LOBBY
Locations nationwide.
Call 405-745-1100 for
your nearest store; ask
for Customer Service.
www.hobbylobby.com
*Discount arts and
crafts stores.*

JOANN FABRICS
Locations nationwide.
Visit www.joann.com for
details of your nearest store.
*A superstore for fabric, craft
materials, patterns, sewing,
and holiday supplies.*

MICHAELS
Locations nationwide.
Visit www.michaels.com for
details of your nearest store.
*A huge selection of every
kind of art and craft material.*

CHRISTMAS TREES

CHRISTMAS TREES, WREATHS, AND DECORATIONS
PO Box 28
Culver, IN 46511
800-458-0445
www.christmas-trees-
    wreaths-decorations.com
*Natural and artificial
Christmas trees, wreaths,
lights, garlands, and topiaries.*

CHRISTMAS LIGHTS

CHRISTMAS LIGHTS, ETC.
4465 Alicia Lane
Building 100
Cumming, GA 30040
www.christmaslightsetc.com
*Offers a wide selection of
lights, wreaths, and lighted
outdoor decorations.*

HOME DEPOT
Locations nationwide.
Visit homedepot.com for
details of your nearest store.
Lights and decorations.

LOWE'S
Locations nationwide.
Visit www.lowes.com for
details of your nearest store.
*Good source of garden
and outdoor lights.*

WAL-MART
Locations nationwide.
501-273-4000
www.walmart.com

CANDLES

CANDLESHTICK
181 Seventh Avenue
New York, NY 10011
212-924-5444
*A wide range of candles
and candle-making supplies.*

ILLUMINATIONS
Mailing address:
1736 Corporate Circle
Petaluma, CA 94954
800-621-2998
www.illuminations.com
*Candles, candle
accessories, and home-
decor products.*

WILLIAMSBURG SOAP AND CANDLE COMPANY
7521 Richmond Road
Williamsburg, VA 23188
757-564-3354
www.candlefactory.com
*This store offers candles
(mostly unscented) in
numerous colors and sizes.*

YANKEE CANDLE COMPANY
PO Box 110
South Deerfield, MA 01373
800-243-1776
www.yankeecandle.com
*This company specializes
in scented candles.*

BEADS, RIBBON, PAPER

HYMAN HENDLER & SONS
67 West 38th Street
New York, NY 10018
212-840-8393
www.hymanhendler.com
*Basic, novelty, and vintage
ribbons. Minimum order $50.*

KATE'S PAPERIE
561 Broadway
New York, NY 10012
212-941-9816
888-809-9880
www.katespaperie.com
*Kate's Paperie carries over
40,000 exotic papers from
around the world.*

M&J TRIMMING
www.mjtrim.com
*Rhinestones, sequined
flowers, ribbons, lace,
rosettes, beaded braid, and
fur and feather trims, all to
buy online.*

PAPYRUS
Stores nationwide.
Visit papyrusonline.com for
details of your nearest store
*Cards, paper, ribbon, gift
wrap, and custom printing.*

PEARL RIVER
477 Broadway
New York, NY 10013
212-431-4770
800-878-2446
www.pearlriver.com
*Colorful, stylish, and
affordable Chinese imports,
including paper decorations
and a wide selection of
origami papers.*

THE RIBBONERIE
191 Potrero Avenue
San Francisco, CA 94103
415-626-6184
www.theribbonerie.com
*This store carries a range
of both domestic and
imported ribbons.*

TINSEL TRADING CO.
47 West 38th Street
New York, NY 10018
212-730-1030
www.tinseltrading.com
*Vintage buttons and beads,
as well as gorgeous silk
and velvet flowers, sequins,
metallic tassels, and
exquisite ribbons.*

templates

advent
calendar

To use the templates, trace the pattern
onto tracing paper and cut out. You can
also photocopy the outlines.

stocking

mobile

templates

card

fairy

table runner

napkin
ring

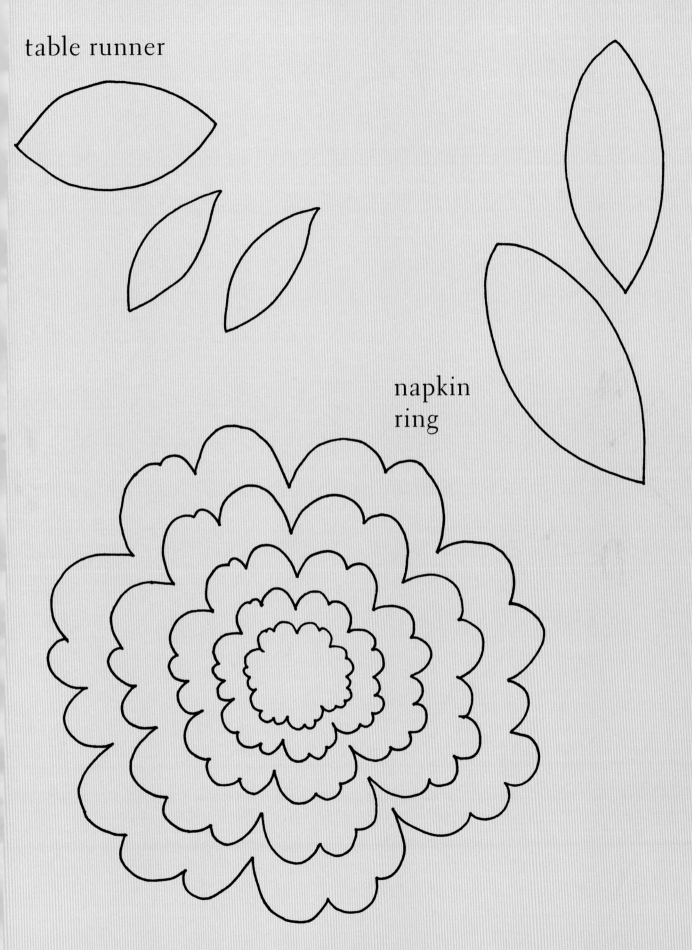

picture credits

Key: ph=photographer, a=above, b=below, r=right, l=left, c=center

All projects by Sania Pell, photographed by Julia Bostock

Endpapers ph Jo Tyler; page 1 ph Carolyn Barber; 2–3 ph Julia Bostock; 4–5 ph Jo Tyler/white sticks from New Covent Garden Market, clear iridescent baubles from The Christmas Shop; 6 ph Caroline Arber/designed and made by Jane Cassini (jane_vintagestyle@yahoo.com) and Ann Brownfield; 8–9 ph Jo Tyler/owner of Adamczewski, Hélène Adamczewski's house in Lewes/socks from Ford Barton; 9 ph Jo Tyler/little buckets from New Covent Garden Market; 10al & 11br ph Jo Tyler/house stylist Clare Nash's home in London/felt from The Cloth Shop, baby socks from Trotters; 10ac ph Caroline Arber/designed and made by Jane Cassini and Ann Brownfield; 10–11a ph Jo Tyler/little buckets from New Covent Garden Market; 10–11b ph Polly Wreford; 11a ph Jo Tyler/tissue paper from Paperchase; 12–13 ph Julia Bostock; 14al ph Sandra Lane; 14–15a ph Jo Tyler/fleece fabric from Boroviks, stockings made by Emily Medley, corduroy fabric from Textile King, wrapping paper from Liberty; 14b ph Jo Tyler/fabric decorations by Caroline Zoob; 15a&b ph Sandra Lane; 16al ph Caroline Arber/stocking by Caroline Zoob; 16ar ph Caroline Arber/stocking made by Jessica Zoob; 16b & 17a ph Jo Tyler/owner of The Swedish Chair, Lena Renkel Eriksson's house in London/paper by Cath Kidston at Liberty, gingham from John Lewis, hessian from New Covent Garden Market; 17b ph Jo Tyler/art director Hans Blomquist's home in London—fabric decorations by Caroline Zoob, etched glass baubles from The Pier; 18–19 ph Julia Bostock; 20 ph Jo Tyler/icicle lights from Woolworths, snowflake decorations from Paperchase; 21 ph Jo Tyler; 22 main ph Jo Tyler/Sally Butler and Tom Carter's house in London, cake stand from Grace & Favour, beeswax sheets from The Hive; 22 inset & 23r ph Sandra Lane; 23l ph David Brittain; 24al ph Jo Tyler/felt bag from Plümo; 24cl ph Jo Tyler/owner of The Swedish Chair, Lena Renkel Eriksson's house in London, white sticks from New Covent Garden Market; 24bl ph Jo Tyler/straw hanging from The Blue Door; 24l ph Jo Tyler/owner of The Swedish Chair, Lena Renkel Eriksson's house in London—furniture from The Swedish Chair, china, table linen, flower vases, bowls, hanging decorations, little men, and checked table linen all from The Blue Door; 25l ph Jo Tyler/red wooden decoration from The Blue Door; 25ar ph Jo Tyler/linen and bowl from The Blue Door; 25cr ph Jo Tyler/fabric decorations by Caroline Zoob; 25br ph Jo Tyler/napkins, china plate, and straw decorations from The Blue Door; 26a all ph Sandra Lane; 26b & 27 ph James Merrell; 28al ph David Brittain; 28ar ph Sandra Lane; 28c ph Jo Tyler/bears and bead trees from Paperchase; 28b ph Jo Tyler/butterflies and beaded garland from V V Rouleaux; 29al ph Emma Lee; 29bl ph Jo Tyler; 29ac ph Polly Wreford/flower and beaded garland candle holder from V V Rouleaux; 29ar ph James Merrell; 29br glass holders from Habitat, mirror from C. Best at Nine Elms Market, Vauxhall; 30–31 ph Julia Bostock; 32 ph Jo Tyler/Sally Butler and Tom Carter's house in London; 33a advent candle from The Blue Door; 33b ph James Merrell; 34al ph Jo Tyler; 34ar ph Jo Tyler/owner of Adamczewski, Hélène Adamczewski's house in Lewes; 34c ph Jo Tyler; 34b ph James Merrell; 35al ph James Merrell; 35ar ph Sandra Lane; 35ac & 35b ph Debi Treloar; 36–37 ph Julia Bostock; 38–39 ph Carolyn Barber; 40l ph Sandra Lane; 40ar ph Polly Wreford; 40br ph Caroline Arber/designed and made by Jane Cassini and Ann Brownfield; 41l ph Jo Tyler/silk flowers from Flowers by Novelty; 41r all ph Carolyn Barber; 42al ph Polly Wreford; 42acl ph Sandra Lane; 42bcl & 42bl ph Carolyn Barber; 42r & 43ar ph Caroline Arber/designed and made by Jane Cassini and Ann Brownfield; 43l ph Carolyn Barber; 43br ph Polly Wreford; 44–45 all ph Carolyn Barber; 46al ph Carolyn Barber; 46l inset ph Polly Wreford; 46b Carolyn Barber; 46ar & 47b ph Caroline Arber/designed and made by Jane Cassini and Ann Brownfield; 47a all ph Polly Wreford; 48–49 ph Julia Bostock; 50a both ph Jo Tyler; 50bl ph Polly Wreford; 55br ph Sandra Lane; 51al&b ph Jo Tyler; 51ac ph Sandra Lane; 51ar ph Polly Wreford; 52 all ph Caroline Arber/designed and made by Jane Cassini and Ann Brownfield; 53 ph Jo Tyler; 54–55 ph Julia Bostock; 56al ph Jo Tyler/snowflake decorations from DZD; 56c ph Jo Tyler; 56r ph Jo Tyler/house stylist Clare Nash's home in London, felt cards made by Emily Medley, cut-glass drops from Paperchase; 56b ph stocking cards by Caroline Zoob; 57 & 58 ph Jo Tyler; 59 ph Sandra Lane; 60 ph Jo Tyler; 61a ph Sandra Lane; 61bl&bc ph Caroline Arber/designed and made by Jane Cassini and Ann Brownfield; 61br ph Jo Tyler; 62l both ph Sandra Lane; 62r & 63br ph Jo Tyler/biscuits made by Clementine Young, gingham ribbon from Temptation Alley; 63al ph Jo Tyler/striped baubles from Paperchase; 63bl ph Jo Tyler; 63ar ph Sandra Lane; 64–65 ph Julia Bostock; 66l ph Sandra Lane; 66r ph Polly Wreford; 67a ph Jo Tyler/basket of baubles from Dawn Gren; 67b all ph Jo Tyler/butterflies and beaded flowers from V V Rouleaux, shell and bird from New Covent Garden Market; 68l both ph Sandra Lane; 68r ph Jo Tyler/robin from New Covent Garden Market, white Christmas tree from DZD; 69 ph Caroline Arber/designed and made by Jane Cassini and Ann Brownfield; 70–71 ph Julia Bostock; 72 ph Jo Tyler/taper candles from Ethos Candles; 73 ph Caroline Arber/designed and made by Jane Cassini and Ann Brownfield; 74al ph Jo Tyler; 74ar&bl ph Sandra Lane; 75a both ph Jo Tyler; 75b ph Sandra Lane; 76a ph Polly Wreford; 76b ph Jo Tyler/candles from Ethos Candles, glasses and glass cake stands from The Dining Room Shop, crackers from Napier Industries; 77l ph Polly Wreford; 77r both ph Sandra Lane; 78–79 ph Julia Bostock; 80al&r ph Sandra Lane; 80cl ph Caroline Arber/designed and made by Jane Cassini and Ann Brownfield; 80b ph Jo Tyler; 81a ph Jo Tyler/china, glass, and linen from Adamczewski; 81b ph Jo Tyler; 82al ph Sandra Lane; 82al, bl&r all ph Sandra Lane; 82cl ph Jo Tyler; 83l, ac, ar&br all ph Sandra Lane; 83bc ph Polly Wreford; 84–85 ph Julia Bostock; 86–87 & 88l ph Jo Tyler; 88r ph Sandra Lane; 89l, ar&br ph James Merrell; 89cr ph Sandra Lane; 90al ph Sandra Lane; 90ac ph Polly Wreford; 90b & 91ac ph Caroline Arber/designed and made by Jane Cassini and Ann Brownfield; 90–91a & 91ar ph Jo Tyler/family home in London, interior design by Vivien Lawrence, beaded wreath from V V Rouleaux; 91b ph James Merrell; 92al ph Jo Tyler/bedspread made by Emily Medley, paper Father Christmas garland from V V Rouleaux; 92bcl ph Jo Tyler/mitten garland from Baileys Home & Garden; 92bl&ar ph Jo Tyler; 93 ph Jo Tyler/family home in London, interior design by Vivien Lawrence, butterflies and beaded garland from V V Rouleaux; 94–95 ph Julia Bostock; 96–97 ph Jo Tyler; 98a all ph Sandra Lane; 98b ph Polly Wreford; 99 ph Jo Tyler/snowflake decorations from Paperchase; 100al&bl ph Sandra Lane; 100cl ph Jo Tyler; 100r ph David Brittain; 101 all ph Sandra Lane; 102a ph Jo Tyler; 102 inset ph Sandra Lane; 102b all ph James Merrell; 103bl ph David Brittain; 103ar ph Polly Wreford; 104–105 ph Julia Bostock; 106 ph Jo Tyler/red wooden decoration from The Blue Door.